DOGS

GREAT DANES

by Elizabeth Andrews

Cody Koala
An Imprint of Pop!
popbooksonline.com

Hello! My name is Cody Koala

This book is filled with videos, puzzles, games, and more! Scan the QR codes* while you read, or visit the website below to make this book pop.

popbooksonline.com/great-dane

*Scanning QR codes requires a web-enabled smart device with a QR code reader app and a camera.

abdobooks.com

Published by Pop!, a division of ABDO, PO Box 398166, Minneapolis, Minnesota 55439.

Printed in the United States of America, North Mankato, Minnesota.

102022
012023

THIS BOOK CONTAINS RECYCLED MATERIALS

Cover Photo: Shutterstock Images
Interior Photos: Shutterstock Images; Getty Images; Alamy Stock Photo
Editor: Grace Hansen
Series Designer: Colleen McLaren

Library of Congress Control Number: 2022941112

Publisher's Cataloging-in-Publication Data
Names: Andrews, Elizabeth, author.
Title: Great danes / by Elizabeth Andrews
Description: Minneapolis, Minnesota : Pop!, 2023 | Series: Dogs | Includes online resources and index.
Identifiers: ISBN 9781098243210 (lib. bdg.) | ISBN 9781098243913 (ebook)
Subjects: LCSH: Great Danes--Juvenile literature. | German mastiff--Juvenile literature. | Sporting dogs--Juvenile literature. | Domestic Dog--Juvenile literature.
Classification: DDC 636.73--dc23

Table of Contents

Chapter 1

Gentle Giants

Great Danes are giants. They tower over most other dogs. On their hind legs, they are taller than most people! But there's no need to fear Great Danes. They are gentle.

Watch a video here!

Great Danes grow to be nearly three feet (.9m) tall. They are big all over. Their legs and tails are long. Their heads are huge. And their paws are the size of human hands!

Even though they are so big, Great Danes love to sit on their owner's lap!

A Great Dane's coat is short and shiny. It can be black, blue, or fawn in color. The coat can also have a pattern. A Great Dane's ears are large and floppy. Sometimes the ears are **cropped**.

harlequin
pattern

fawn

black

blue

Chapter 2

Personality

Great Danes were originally **bred** to be guard dogs. Over the years, their protective **instincts** have faded. Now, they are loving and goofy dogs that can fit in with any family.

Learn more here!

Great Danes are somewhat playful. But they would rather stretch out on a couch or bed. They should be taken on daily walks for exercise. They will easily make friends while out and about!

Great Danes show love by leaning their heavy bodies on their people.

Chapter 3

Dog Care

Great Danes are very big dogs. They have one of the shortest lifespans of any **breed** due to their size. A whole lot of love is fit into their seven to ten years.

A Great Dane named Zeus holds the record for the tallest dog in the world.

Explore links here!

Great Danes eat a lot. It is important to feed them healthy food. Their bowls need to be raised. This way, Great Danes do not have to bend down to reach their food and water.

A Great Dane's coat only requires occasional brushing and monthly baths. It's important to have a

good relationship with a vet. Regular checkups will keep Great Danes healthier for longer.

Chapter 4

Puppies

Great Danes are born at just over one pound (.45kg). When they are ready to be **adopted**, they can be almost 30 lbs (13.6kg)! Training should start before they get too big to handle.

Complete an activity here!

Making Connections

Text-to-Self

Would you want to have a dog as big as the Great Dane? Explain why or why not.

Text-to-Text

Have you read any books about other large dog breeds? Did they have anything in common with Great Danes?

Text-to-World

A Great Dane holds the record for World's Tallest Dog. Do you know of any other world records a dog has?

Glossary

adopted – taken in as a pet.

bred – developed to act and look a specific way, or serve a certain purpose.

breed – a particular type or kind of animal.

cropped – having part or all of the flaps of a dog's ears removed in a surgery.

instinct – natural behavior in an animal that is not taught but is simply part of what an animal is born with.

Index

Online Resources

popbooksonline.com

Thanks for reading this Cody Koala book!

This book is filled with videos, puzzles, games, and more! Scan the QR codes* while you read, or visit the website below to make this book pop.

popbooksonline.com/great-dane

*Scanning QR codes requires a web-enabled smart device with a QR code reader app and a camera.